Food
CARROTS

Louise Spilsbury

Heinemann
LIBRARY

www.heinemann.co.uk/library
Visit our website to find out more information about Heinemann Library books.

To order:
 Phone 44 (0) 1865 888066
 Send a fax to 44 (0) 1865 314091
Visit the Heinemann Bookshop at www.heinemann.co.uk/library to browse our catalogue and order online.

First published in Great Britain by Heinemann Library,
Halley Court, Jordan Hill, Oxford OX2 8EJ
a division of Reed Educational and Professional Publishing Ltd.
Heinemann is a registered trademark of Reed Educational and Professional Publishing Ltd.

OXFORD MELBOURNE AUCKLAND
JOHANNESBURG BLANTYRE GABORONE
IBADAN PORTSMOUTH (NH) USA CHICAGO

Designed by Celia Floyd
Illustrated by Alan Fraser
Originated by Ambassador Litho Ltd
Printed in Hong Kong/China by South China Printing Co.

ISBN 0 431 12771 9 (hardback)
06 05 04 03 02
10 9 8 7 6 5 4 3 2 1

British Library Cataloguing in Publication Data
Spilsbury, Louise
   Carrots. – (Food)
   1. Carrots 2. Juvenile literature
   I. Title
   641.3'513

Acknowledgements
The Publishers would like to thank the following for permission to reproduce photographs:
Bridgeman Art Library: pp.8, 9; Corbis: pp.7, 10, 24, 25; FPG International: p.18; Holt Studios International: pp.5, 11, 14, 16, 19; Imagebank: pp.13, 20; Liz Eddison: pp. 4, 21, 23, 28 (left and right), 29 (top and bottom); Martin Caunce/P. Caunce and Son: p.15; Corbis: p.12; Stone: p.17; Thompson & Morgan (UK) Ltd: p6; Trevor Clifford: p.22.

Cover photograph reproduced with permission of Gareth Boden.

Every effort has been made to contact copyright holders of any material reproduced in this book.
Any omissions will be rectified in subsequent printings if notice is given to the Publishers.

CONTENTS

Words written in bold, **like this**, are explained in the Glossary.

WHAT ARE CARROTS?

Carrots are a kind of **vegetable**. A vegetable is a part of a plant you can eat. You can eat carrots **raw** (uncooked) or cooked.

Carrots grow on carrot plants. You cannot see carrots growing. They are a part of the plant that grows under the ground.

KINDS OF CARROTS

Carrots come in many sizes, shapes and colours. There are round, fat, small, long and thin carrots. There are white, yellow and purple kinds.

Most people eat long orange carrots. These were first grown in Holland 400 years ago. Now they are popular across the world.

IN THE PAST

Many **Romans** believed that eating carrots made stomach aches better. They also thought carrots helped them to see at night.

Carrots became very popular in Europe 500 years ago. Most people ate the carrots. Some decorated their hats with the feathery leaves!

AROUND THE WORLD

Carrots grow best in countries where it is not too hot or too cold. This farmer in Ecuador grows carrots for her family to eat.

This huge carrot farm is in California, USA. Some carrots grown here are sold in America and some are **exported** (sold to other countries).

LOOKING AT CARROTS

Carrots grow from **seeds**. In the soil, the seeds start to grow. **Shoots** grow upwards towards the light. **Roots** grow down into the soil.

Carrots are a kind of root. As they grow down into the soil they get fatter and longer. Tall, fluffy leaves form on the shoots.

GROWING CARROTS

Carrots grow best in loose soil. That is why farmers use a **plough** to break up the soil before they put the **seeds** into the ground.

This farmer is using a machine called
a planter. It drops seeds into the soil.
It spaces the seeds out so the plants
have room to grow.

SPRAYING AND DIGGING

Farmers need to protect carrot plants from **diseases** and **pests**. Some farmers put special sprays on the plants to stop them being damaged.

When the carrots are big enough to eat, farmers dig them up. They use a machine that pulls up the carrot plants. It also cuts off the leaves.

WASHING AND CHECKING

A truck takes the carrots to a **packing house**. The carrots go into a machine that cleans them. Water washes the soil off the carrots.

The carrots go on to a **conveyor belt**. Workers check them. They throw away any carrots that are bad, split or broken.

CARROTS TO US

Then a machine sorts the carrots into different sizes. They are moved in large crates, bags or boxes. Lorries take the carrots to the shops.

Some carrots are sold with the leaves on. Some carrots are **frozen** or packed into cans with salt and water. These keep longer than fresh carrots.

EATING CARROTS

Most people cut off the carrot skin before they eat them. Others eat the skin as well. You should wash carrots well before you eat them.

Carrots are used in soups and stews, and in cakes and puddings. Carrots are also used to make food **products**, such as carrot juice.

GOOD FOR YOU

Carrots contain a lot of **Vitamin** A. This vitamin helps to keep your skin and bones healthy. It also helps your body fight **disease**.

Carrots also contain **fibre**. Fibre is a part of some foods that passes through your body when you eat it. It helps keep your body healthy.

HEALTHY EATING

You need to eat different kinds of food to keep you well. This food pyramid shows you how much of each different food you need.

You should eat some of the things at the bottom and in the middle of the pyramid every day.

Sweet foods are at the top of the pyramid. Try not to eat too much of these sweet foods!

The food in each part of the pyramid helps your body in different ways.

Carrots belong in the middle of the pyramid.

Cakes, sweets, **fats**, oils and honey

Milk, yoghurt and cheese

Meat, fish, eggs and nuts

Vegetables

Fruit

Bread, **cereals**, rice and pasta

27

VEGETABLE SPREAD RECIPE

1 Peel the carrots and then grate them. Ask an adult to help you do this with a hand grater or in a food processor.

2 Now grate the courgette in the same way. (You do not need to peel the courgette first.)

3 Put the grated carrot and courgette into a bowl with the cream cheese.

4 Chop the parsley carefully and mix it in with the other things. Add a little pepper as well, if you like it.

5 Put the bowl in a fridge to chill. Then you can eat this spread on crackers, toast or bagels.

GLOSSARY

cereals breakfast foods are called cereals because they are made from cereal plants, like wheat and rice

conveyor belt moving belt that takes things placed on it from one place to another

diseases diseases can harm people, other animals and plants

exported when something is grown or made in one country but taken to another country to be sold

fats type of food. Butter, oil and margarine are kinds of fat. It is not healthy to eat too much fat.

fibre part of a plant that passes through our bodies when we eat it

frozen when food is kept as cold as ice to keep it fresh

packing house building where vegetables are cleaned, sorted and packed

pests insects that can damage plants

plough machine that breaks up soil to make it ready for planting seeds

product something that is made to be sold

raw not cooked

Romans Romans ruled over many lands, including Britain and much of the rest of Europe for about 920 years (from 510 BC to AD 410)

roots plant parts that grow down into the ground. They take in water from the soil for the plant.

seed part of a plant used to grow more plants

shoot first stem and leaves of a new plant

vegetable part of a plant that we can eat. Carrots, potatoes, peas and lettuce are kinds of vegetables.

vitamin kind of goodness that is in certain foods. Vitamins help us grow and protect our bodies from illness.

MORE BOOKS TO READ

Plants: How Plants Grow, Angela Royston,
  Heinemann Library, 1999

Safe and Sound: Eat Well, Angela Royston,
  Heinemann Library, 1999

Senses: Tasting, Karen Hartley, Chris Macro,
  Phillip Taylor, Heinemann Library, 2000

The Senses: Taste, Mandy Suhr, Hodder Wayland, 1994

INDEX

Titles in the *Food* series include:

Hardback   0 431 12770 0

Hardback   0 431 12700 X

Hardback   0 431 12771 9

Hardback   0 431 12702 6

Hardback   0 431 12706 9

Hardback   0 431 12701 8

Hardback   0 431 12772 7

Hardback   0 431 12773 5

Find out about the other titles in this series on our website www.heinemann.co.uk/library